D1231908

COOL CATS

Cornish Rexes

by Christina Leighton

BELLWETHER MEDIA • MINNEAPOLIS, MN

BLASTOFF!
2
READERS

Note to Librarians, Teachers, and Parents:

Blastoff! Readers are carefully developed by literacy experts and combine standards-based content with developmentally appropriate text.

Level 1 provides the most support through repetition of high-frequency words, light text, predictable sentence patterns, and strong visual support.

Level 2 offers early readers a bit more challenge through varied simple sentences, increased text load, and less repetition of high-frequency words.

Level 3 advances early-fluent readers toward fluency through increased text and concept load, less reliance on visuals, longer sentences, and more literary language.

Level 4 builds reading stamina by providing more text per page, increased use of punctuation, greater variation in sentence patterns, and increasingly challenging vocabulary.

Level 5 encourages children to move from "learning to read" to "reading to learn" by providing even more text, varied writing styles, and less familiar topics.

Whichever book is right for your reader, Blastoff! Readers are the perfect books to build confidence and encourage a love of reading that will last a lifetime!

This edition first published in 2017 by Bellwether Media, Inc.

No part of this publication may be reproduced in whole or in part without written permission of the publisher. For information regarding permission, write to Bellwether Media, Inc., Attention: Permissions Department, 5357 Penn Avenue South, Minneapolis, MN 55419.

Library of Congress Cataloging-in-Publication Data

Names: Leighton, Christina, author.
Title: Cornish Rexes / by Christina Leighton.
Other titles: Blastoff! Readers. 2, Cool Cats.
Description: Minneapolis, MN : Bellwether Media, Inc., [2017] | Series:
   Blastoff! Readers. Cool Cats | Audience: Ages 5-8. | Audience: K to grade 3.
   Includes bibliographical references and index.
Identifiers: LCCN 2015048437 | ISBN 9781626173965 (hardcover : alk. paper)
Subjects: LCSH: Rex cat–Juvenile literature. | Cat breeds–Juvenile
   literature.
Classification: LCC SF449.R4 L45 2017 | DDC 636.8/22–dc23
LC record available at http://lccn.loc.gov/2015048437

Printed in the United States of America, North Mankato, MN.

Table of Contents

What Are Cornish Rexes?

Cornish rexes are short-haired cats. They have curly **coats**!

They are soft like rabbits.
Part of their name comes
from rex rabbits.

5

These cats have egg-shaped heads.
Their big ears sit high. They have
thin bodies and **arched** backs.

Cornish Rex Profile

egg-shaped head

arched back

curly coat

long legs

Weight: 5 to 10 pounds (2 to 4.5 kilograms)

Life Span: 11 to 15 years

History of Cornish Rexes

Cornish rexes are from Cornwall, England. In 1950, a cream-colored kitten named Kallibunker was born there.

England

W N E S

Cornwall

His hair was curly! He looked like a little lamb.

Kallibunker's owner **bred** him to make more curly-haired cats.

His kittens helped the new **breed** grow.

Cornish rex coats come in many colors and patterns.

Cornish Rex Coats

solid

pointed

tabby

tortoiseshell

Some coats are **solid** or **pointed**. Others are **tabby** or **tortoiseshell**.

The breed has long legs and tails. They look **elegant**.

Some people say they are the **runway models** of the cat world.

Cornish rexes are smart and full of energy. They love to play fetch.

They bounce off walls and speed after toys. Some can even open doors!

17

These cats are **affectionate**.
They like to be hugged by
their owners.

Many claim laps to cuddle.
Others enjoy shoulder rides.

Cornish rexes rest in the sun.
Some keep warm under blankets.

Soon it is time to play again!

Glossary

affectionate–loving

arched–curved

bred–purposely mated two cats to make kittens with certain qualities

breed–a type of cat

coats–the hair or fur covering some animals

elegant–having grace and beauty

pointed–having dark fur at certain points; pointed cats have dark faces, ears, legs, and tails.

runway models–people who walk down long paths to show an audience clothing

solid–one color

tabby–a pattern that has stripes, patches, or swirls of colors

tortoiseshell–a pattern of yellow, orange, and black with few or no patches of white

To Learn More

AT THE LIBRARY

Leaf, Christina. *Devon Rexes.* Minneapolis, Minn.: Bellwether Media, 2016.

Murray, Julie. *Cornish Rex Cats.* Edina, Minn.: ABDO Pub., 2003.

Sexton, Colleen. *The Life Cycle of a Cat.* Minneapolis, Minn.: Bellwether Media, 2011.

ON THE WEB

Learning more about Cornish rexes is as easy as 1, 2, 3.

1. Go to www.factsurfer.com.

2. Enter "Cornish rexes" into the search box.

3. Click the "Surf" button and you will see a list of related web sites.

With factsurfer.com, finding more information is just a click away.

Index

The images in this book are reproduced through the courtesy of: Eric Isselee, front cover, p. 5; Imageman, p. 4; SuperStock/ Glow Images, p. 6; Jagodka, p. 7; skyfish, p. 9 (background); j-paul, p. 9 (subject); Oleg Kozlov, p. 10; Jean-Michel Labat/ ardea.co/ Pantheon/ SuperStock, pp. 11, 13 (bottom right); Olena Lyzun, pp. 12-13; DragoNika, p. 13 (bottom left); Labat-Rouquette/ Kimball Stock, p. 14; Fedir Shulenok, pp. 13 (top left), 15; Alena Kazlouskaya, p. 13 (top right); Liliya Kulianionak, pp. 16, 20; Erik Lam, p. 17; Shelli Jensen, p. 18 (background); Luna K, p. 18 (subject); zhu difeng, p. 19 (background); Svetlana Mihailova, pp. 19 (subject), 21.